Original title:
Forest Floor Fantasies

Copyright © 2025 Creative Arts Management OÜ
All rights reserved.

Author: Elliot Harrison
ISBN HARDBACK: 978-1-80567-163-3
ISBN PAPERBACK: 978-1-80567-462-7

The Hidden Quest of the Leaf-Cutter

In a world where ants parade,
With tiny scissors, unafraid,
They snip and clip with crafty glee,
Tiny warriors, brave and free.

A crumb of sandwich, left behind,
An epic feast, they have in mind.
On picnic blankets, laughter sings,
While ants debate on leafy things.

With cardboard helmets, made of dust,
They charge ahead, do what they must.
Their queen awaits, her bounty grand,
They scurry off—it's all well planned!

Yet on their route, a spider looms,
With webs like traps and plans for dooms.
But silly ants just dance away,
Pretend it's just another day!

So prance and play, you miniature crew,
In the grass, you'll find adventures new.
Your quest is odd, but oh, so bright,
In this grand saga, you own the night!

The Gardens of the Subterranean

Underneath the leafy crown,
Worms throw parties, shaking down.
Mice in tuxedos toss confetti,
Cakes made of crumbs, oh so petty.

Bugs tap dance on the mushroom caps,
Ants in line do fancy laps.
Toadstools serve a punch of juice,
While snails are slow, but cut loose.

Creatures of the Softening Glade

Where the gnomes run wild and free,
Ogres juggle, one, two, three.
Frogs in bow ties croak a tune,
While fairy lights dance 'neath the moon.

Squirrels compete in acorn toss,
Whimsical games that never gloss.
Rabbits sport hats with charm and flair,
All join in, none a care.

Wandering Through Nature's Palette

Colors drip from a brush held high,
With splashes bright, oh my, oh my!
Bees don capes, take to the sky,
As flowers giggle, oh so spry.

A painter snail draws in the air,
With laughter sweet, a joyous flare.
Chirping crickets recite their verse,
Nature's stage, oh how diverse!

Reveries of the Hidden Habitat

Badgers in drama, stealing the show,
Playing charades, they steal the glow.
Foxes play tricks, oh what a jest,
In this nook, they know no rest.

Owls gossip deep with a hoot and a wink,
Sipping on dew like it's the drink.
Nature's jesters, forever they play,
In a world where fun runs all day.

Serenades from the Earth's Lappet

Squirrels dance in silly twirls,
Their acorns roll like little pearls.
Fungi giggle, wear a grin,
While grumpy toads just seldom win.

Bugs in bow ties waltz around,
As bees hum sweetly, quite profound.
Worms in top hats dig with flair,
Each root a thrill, a giggle, rare.

The Charm of Timeworn Leaves

Leaves in hues of yellow, red,
Plotting mischief, so it's said.
They rustle whispers, tales of yore,
As ghosts of trees add to the lore.

Fallen twigs hold secret chats,
About the antics of the bats.
A leaf named Larry, quite the clown,
Winds up wearing a cap upside down.

Magic of the Sundrenched Shade

Beneath the sun, the shadows play,
Creating dance floors where critters sway.
Mice in overalls groove in time,
While butterflies sip tea with lime.

The sunbeams tickle grass so green,
Awkward ants form a conga scene.
Chubby rabbits hop without care,
Each bounce revealing fluffy underwear.

Foraging Through the Fabled Depths

In tangled vines, adventures sprout,
Each leafy path's a silly route.
Raccoons rave at midnight shows,
While hedgehogs boast of poker pros.

Digging deep, a twisty maze,
Caterpillars throw leafy plays.
Finding snacks in hidden nooks,
Read the funniest of storybooks.

Whispers Among the Roots

The mushrooms giggle, sprouting wide,
As ants parade, all filled with pride.
A snail in sunglasses takes a stroll,
While beetles plot a rock and roll.

The earthworms waltz beneath the ground,
Chasing shadows, round and round.
A fox with specs reads tales of lore,
And everyone's laughing—what a floor!

Treetop Shadows Dance

The squirrels toss acorns with great flair,
As owl judges children in midair.
With leafy hats and twiggy bows,
A dance-off ensues beneath the crows.

The branches laugh at the clumsy bee,
Who missed the mark on a wild spree.
The breezy giggles tickle the leaves,
As sunlight plays through all the eaves.

Beneath the Canopy's Embrace

A raccoon steals snacks, thinks he's real sly,
While chipmunks giggle as they pass by.
The shadows whisper tales but all miss,
Pouring rain just can't dampen the bliss.

The ferns wear hats made of dew,
As the pollen floats like clouds, it's true.
And here's a secret: the mushrooms sing,
Under the xylophone's woodsy ring.

Secrets of the Lush Understory

The beetles have meetings, discussing the day,
While caterpillars argue about what to say.
A hedgehog giggles at the chaos unfurl,
In a world where even mushrooms twirl.

The spiders knit webs with threads of laughter,
While fireflies blink like lights in a drafter.
The tales they weave are tall and bright,
In the tickling twilight, oh what a sight!

Wonderment Beneath the Green Veil

In shadows where the critters play,
The mushrooms dance and sway all day.
A squirrel dreams of becoming a star,
While beetles boast of trips near and far.

The ants parade with tiny brass bands,
Humor found in their tiny plans.
A worm recites poetry so divine,
While nearby, snails sip grape juice from a vine.

Imprints of Life Among Starlit Ferns

A raccoon juggles acorns with flair,
While owls giggle, hanging in mid-air.
Frogs play leapfrog, they're quite the sight,
Underneath the glow of the soft moonlight.

Grasshoppers sing in a chirpy choir,
Competing with crickets, never to tire.
Fireflies compete in a glowing race,
Their flickering lights all over the place.

The Covenant of Shadows and Sprouts

Where shadows laugh and sprout like weeds,
A hedgehog ponders his fashion needs.
A rabbit snickers, playing hide-and-seek,
As mushrooms argue who's the best at cheek.

Twirling ferns play a silly charade,
While beetles dance in a wiggly parade.
The breeze carries giggles, a whimsical sound,
As creatures unite, in joy they abound.

Hidden Adventures in Twilight's Fern

Under twilight where secrets unfold,
A shy lizard tells stories so bold.
Ladybugs dress up for costume night,
While spiders weave tales that take flight.

Tails of raccoons swing through fronds,
Jumping through shadows like superheroes' bonds.
With laughter and frolic, they roam and they play,
In secret adventures as night turns to day.

Dreams Weaved in Twigs and Thorns

In a tangle of twigs, dreams start to sprout,
A squirrel in pajamas, with acorns about.
He holds a grand party, all critters are seen,
Dancing to nutty tunes, oh what a scene!

The frogs wear fine hats, the ants bring the cheese,
A caterpillar DJ moves with such ease.
With laughter and giggles, the night drifts away,
As shadows play tricks, under stars they will sway.

Echoes of Sprites in Decay

Beneath the old branches where fairies do dwell,
They giggle and cackle, casting their spell.
But alas! Their wings snag on thorns of the past,
Their sprightly giggles may be fading fast.

A worm starts a rumor, 'The sprites aren't so bright!'
While beetles roll by with a chuckle in flight.
They throw tiny tantrums, quite proud of their mess,
But even in chaos, they're still quite the dress!

Sunbeams through the Verdant Veil

Bright light filters down, through leaves it cascades,
Where mushrooms wear hats and dance in parades.
A bunny on stilts hops with great delight,
While shadows play hide-and-seek, a comical sight!

The daisies all giggle, the ferns sway in cheer,
As sunbeam confetti falls down through the years.
Each moment's a party, and oh what a game,
Where even the sun feels a little bit lame!

The Symphony of Soil and Stone

Dig deeper, dig deeper, the moles sing their tune,
While worms form a band 'neath the light of the moon.
Crickets compose, under starry commands,
A maraca of pebbles in their wiggly hands.

The stones start to boulder, their rhythm is strong,
As daisies join in with a sweet little song.
Together they dance on this mischievous stage,
As squirrels take a bow, feeling quite sage!

Lurking Magic of the Subterranean

Down in the dirt, the gnomes conspire,
With wiggly worms and a mad desire.
A squirrel's tail twitches, a dance so tight,
They giggle and wiggle, oh what a sight!

Moles wear hats that are far too small,
Hopping on mushrooms, they rise and fall.
Toadstools bob like tiny boats,
Full of silly dreams and curious quotes.

Meditations Among the Whispering Weeds

Beneath the flowers, rabbits sing,
Playing hopscotch with a cheerful spring.
The daisies gossip, the clovers laugh,
While ants debate their afternoon path.

A ladybug winks in polka dots,
Sipping dew from where the sun blots.
In the realm of fluff, where giggles soar,
Weeds hold wisdom in their uproar.

Dreamscapes Beneath the Canopy

In the shadows where shadows are deep,
Frogs wear pajamas, ready for sleep.
Bamboo flutes play a lullaby tune,
Even the stars peek out by the moon.

Beetles are breakdancing on moist logs,
While fireflies pop like sparkling cogs.
The branches are laughing, a vibrant cheer,
Dancing together, from far and near.

The Mosaic of Shelter in Nature's Arms

Pine cones gather for a concert show,
While chipmunks cheer, their excitement aglow.
Barking at squirrels who stole their keys,
Nature's humor flies on the breeze.

Leaves giggle softly, sharing their tales,
Frolicking under the moonlight trails.
In a world where nonsense makes some sense,
Hilarity reigns, as it so intense!

Adventures in the Sweet Decay

Among the fallen leaves we leap,
Where mushrooms wear their polka dots,
Squirrels dance and squirrels peep,
As acorns roll like little pots.

In sunlit glades, the snails parade,
With tiny hats and mismatched socks,
They munch on greens, all unafraid,
While crickets plot their laughing talks.

The grasshoppers hum a silly tune,
As bumblebees do wobble-waltz,
A curious raccoon with a spoon,
Steals berries and he does not halt.

Each step a crunch, a giggle bursts,
We tiptoe past a sleeping toad,
In this strange land where laughter thirsts,
We'll make silly songs our abode.

Beneath the Surface: A Living Text

Underneath the leafy quilt,
The ants play cards with twigs and leaves,
A gopher sneezes, what a jilt!
He wonders now what little thieves.

Mice in boots take joyous leaps,
While fungi sit and roll their eyes,
A worm competes in storytelling heaps,
Claiming it's the fanciest prize.

Amidst the roots where shadows creep,
Crickets sing of wild ballet,
A fox in tights, he cannot keep,
From tripping as he makes his play.

Here game's afoot and fun is rife,
In stories spun with twisted glee,
Each tunnel's a new urban life,
Where every twist is pure esprit.

Nature's Forgotten Tapestry

Bumble blooms in bright array,
With slapstick bees that miss their flight,
A ladybug lost on her way,
Finds solace in a spider's light.

The moss is soft, a couch of dreams,
Yet frogs jump high to steal the show,
Where laughter leads to silly schemes,
And soft winds hum like old-time flow.

The thistle bears a witty smile,
As hedgehogs don their spiny hats,
They spin and twirl in forest style,
While beetles boast of acorn chats.

A tapestry of giggles we weave,
With creatures prancing to and fro,
In every nook, they do believe,
This realm is where the wonders glow.

Chronicles of the Thicket's Heart

In thickets deep, the stories hide,
A raccoon juggles twigs and seeds,
While owls hoot with eyes so wide,
Plotting out their mischief leads.

A hedgehog rolls in leaves of gold,
With dreams of sweets—oh what a dare!
He claims to be the bravest bold,
Yet squeaks around the curious stare.

In this wild nook, where laughter thrives,
The bushes whisper secrets dear,
While foxes spin yarns with high-fives,
And every giggle stirs the cheer.

These chronicles of uproar loud,
Paint joyful scenes of silly plots,
Where nature wears her playful shroud,
And every heart earns tricks and knots.

The Melodic Murmur of Soil

In the dirt, a worm lets out a tune,
Singing loudly to a lazy raccoon.
The beetles tap dance, what a sight,
Underneath the stars, oh what a night!

A snail steals the mic, slow but clear,
While ants form a band, bringing the cheer.
With mushrooms as lights, they jam on cue,
Even gophers groove to this earthy brew!

Buried Colors of the Verdant World

Colors peek through the deep, dark brown,
A blue jay's wiggle makes others frown.
With dandelions dressed in sunny cheer,
A tumbleweed rolls through, bringing good beer!

Shades of purple where the violets bloom,
A squirrel's tail twitches with the joy to zoom.
Rainbow roots, the onions giggle,
As a hedgehog flops in a colorful wiggle!

Sprouts of Imagination in the Gloom

Underneath the ferns, a story's spun,
About a lizard that thought she could run.
Mice knit tiny sweaters for the cold,
While crickets fashion shoes, shining gold!

An owl wears glasses, looking quite wise,
While fireflies flash, no need for disguise.
In silly hats, they gather around,
With tales of mischief in shadows abound!

Portraits of Dust and Dappled Light

Dust bunnies laugh, they take to the stage,
Joking 'bout clumsiness, acting their age.
A shadowy fox sends a wink their way,
Saying, 'Join me, friends, let's dance and sway!'

The sun peeks in, casting stripes on the ground,
A dappled expression where joy can be found.
With twigs as guitars and leaves for a hat,
Together they strum in a merry old spat!

Beneath the Bark

A squirrel in a tuxedo sings,
Wearing acorn hats with tiny wings.
The mushrooms laugh, all dressed in spots,
As flowers dance and tumble in knots.

The trees all giggle, tickled by breeze,
While ants march, hoping to join the tease.
A beetle jives on a clover hill,
His two left feet give everyone a thrill.

Dreams Unwind

A snail proposes a race with a mouse,
They laugh and play around the house.
The ladybugs cheer with tiny signs,
While grasshoppers leap on twisted vines.

The moon shines bright, a wink from above,
As crickets croon sweet songs of love.
The owls chuckle in the night so clear,
While shadows play hide and seek with fear.

Dances of the Hidden Creatures

Little creatures in a disco scene,
Grooving under leaves so lush and green.
Fireflies flash like disco balls,
While every beetle struts and sprawls.

Butterflies twirl in a colorful spree,
While a worm attempts a grand plié.
The ferns sway gently, tapping their toes,
As the earth beneath them hums and glows.

Mossy Dreams and Fern Fragments

On mossy cushions, gnomes craft their hats,
With whimsical patterns of whiskers and bats.
They sip sweet nectar from purple blooms,
Swapping tales that sway like the fumes.

The ferns giggle, tickling the toes,
Of weary travelers who stumble and doze.
While tiny spiders weave jokes in silk,
Creating laughter with threads more than milk.

Enchanted Roots in Twilight's Lair

Roots wiggle and jive, what a curious sight,
As shadows grow longer, fading sunlight.
A hedgehog sports shades, oh what a flair,
While mice share secrets born from thin air.

The twilight hums with mischievous dreams,
As shadows dance under silver moon beams.
A raccoon with a crown begins to decree,
This dance party's just for you and me!

Murmurs of Nature's Innocence

In the shade, ants hold court,
Debating crumbs like fine report.
Beetles don their tiny hats,
While snails race by in slow chats.

Squirrels giggle up in trees,
Stealing acorns, a feast with ease.
A frog croaks, it's quite a show,
In a leap, it steals the flow.

Mice in masks throw a grand ball,
With petals twirling, they stand tall.
While fireflies flicker, a dance begins,
To the tune of the wind, where laughter spins.

Underneath this leafy spread,
The stories tease, they're never dead.
Nature laughs with twinkling eyes,
In the heart where mischief lies.

The Language of Leaf-Litter Dreams

Amid the leaves, whispers abound,
Where critters play upon the ground.
A raccoon rehearses its grand heist,
While mushrooms gossip, not very nice.

Each acorn tells of plans turned wild,
As the wind coaxes laughter, beguiled.
A wily fox wears a grin so sly,
As he plots under a watchful sky.

Chipmunks swap stories, quite absurd,
Of daring deeds that seem unheard.
While the breeze chimes in, a jester too,
Creating laughter, both old and new.

A conga line of bugs takes flight,
In their tiny world, it feels just right.
With rhythm pulsing through each groove,
In a dance, nature finds its move.

Ciphers Between the Roots and Spores

In tangles where the shadows play,
Mushrooms hide in a silly way.
Lichens giggle on rock and tree,
Whispering secrets, wild and free.

Roots weave stories beneath the earth,
Of births, rebirths, and nature's mirth.
Worms with wit debate their fate,
Charming tales, they can't be late.

A snail picks up the pace to tease,
While drizzle drips from leafy leaves.
The sun peeks through in cheery bits,
Painting smiles on all its fits.

Amid compost, dreams take flight,
An orchestra of bugs at night.
Nature's play, a comical spree,
In every nook, joy runs wild and free.

Serene Undertones in Nature's Palette

Underneath a canopy so bright,
Birds chat in hues of sheer delight.
While hedgehogs roll in carefree fun,
Chasing shadows under the sun.

Ducks don quacks in a fancy tune,
As they paddle, a jovial swoon.
With splashes flying, all in jest,
They claim this pond, their very nest.

The breeze carries songs, a light-hearted joke,
Where flowers giggle, all finely bespoke.
An orchestra of sounds in sync,
Tickles the ears, making hearts wink.

Squirrels throw acorns, a playful fight,
While shadows dance under the twilight.
In this realm where laughter's stored,
Every heartbeat finds its accord.

The Language of Seeds and Ferns

A tiny seed spoke to a fern,
"Let's twist and twirl, it's your turn!"
The fern just waved, said, "Not today,"
"I'm busy with curls in a leafy ballet."

The mushrooms chuckled, missed the charm,
"I hope you don't sprout and cause alarm!"
The acorns giggled, they're quite the crowd,
"But we'll bring snacks, let's party loud!"

Grasshoppers leaped, joining the fuss,
Said, "You can't talk, just ride the bus!"
Seeds whispered tales, all went awry,
While ferns shot glances, a leafy sigh.

And so they danced in the green delight,
Flipping and flopping from day to night.
In the chatty glade, laughter spread,
With seeds and ferns, the fun's widespread!

A Tapestry of Fallen Petals

Petals fell like confetti from trees,
Each one promised its own tiny tease.
They gathered in heaps, a colorful mound,
"Who's ready for fun?!" the petals all crowned.

A ladybug joined with jazz on the scene,
Said, "Watch me boogie, I'm light and lean!"
But the petals all slipped and tumbled around,
Rolling and giggling, a petal-glow pound.

"Let's play hide and seek among the greens!"
Cried the bluebells, giggling their means.
But the roses chimed in, "We're just too shy,"
And daisies joked, "We must surely fly!"

So swirled in the air, a colorful mess,
A tapestry woven with sweet cheerfulness.
Blowing on breezes, off they did blow,
Leaving behind tales of giggles and glow!

Moonlit Dances of the Woodland

Under the moon, where shadows tease,
Creatures emerged, as graceful as leaves.
The owls took flight, in swirling delight,
"Join us, dear friends, for a magical night!"

A raccoon wore masks, prancing with flair,
"Look at these moves! I've nonchalance rare!"
Toadstools clapped, keeping the beat,
While fireflies danced on dainty feet.

Squirrels brought snacks, a nibble or two,
"Is this moon light or just me and you?"
Chirps and chuckles drifted on air,
As woodland friends jiggle without a care.

The stars winked down, joining the song,
It felt like the night couldn't last too long.
With laughter echoing through every glen,
They spun and twirled just to start again!

In the Heart of the Green Abyss

Deep in the woods, where the humor grows,
Lived a walrus who wore silly clothes.
He'd waddle about, mischief his game,
Chasing the rabbits, but it's all the same.

With ferns as his backdrop, he made a stand,
"Why wear any pants when you've got a band?"
The gnomes laughed loud, shaking their heads,
"Walrus, oh, stop! You'll wake all the beds!"

A chatty fox nibbled on berries near,
"Dance while you can! Just don't shed a tear!"
While bees buzzed along with their own little tune,
The pitch of their hum could rival the moon.

And in this green abyss, so strange yet fair,
Life danced to rhythms that filled the air.
So with giggles and banter, forever we sway,
In the heart of green fun, having a play!

Hidden Reveries Among the Roots

In the shade where shadows play,
Little critters dance away.
A squirrel tells a joke or two,
While a worm laughs, 'What's a tree to you?'

Underneath the emerald throne,
Snails are racing, seeds are sown.
A beetle thinks he's quite the star,
While mushrooms giggle, near and far.

Ants march by, a jolly band,
Laying bricks—a castle planned.
And what's this? A rogue shoe's found!
As nature giggles all around.

Beneath the roots, the stories grow,
Of silly seeds and cheeky show.
In every nook, a secret cheer,
Where whispers tease and fun is near.

The Allure of Dappled Sunlight

Sunlight dips like a playful cat,
Winking at leaves, 'Imagine that!'
A butterfly dons a polka dot,
And says, 'I'm great—like it or not!'

Dappled beams like a child's toy,
Bringing laughter, spreading joy.
The squirrel's fur, a sheen of gold,
Tells tales of mischief, brave and bold.

Rabbits prance with gleeful zest,
In playtime games, they're at their best.
The shadows chuckle in delight,
As daydreams twirl in goofy flight.

In glimmers soft, the antics lay,
Where sunlight's charm will always play.
With every beam, a story spun,
In laughter, life has just begun!

Tales Written in the City of Fungus

In a nook where fungi bloom,
A toadstool chef stirs hearty stew.
With a cap upon his head so grand,
He claims, 'I'm the finest in the land!'

Mushrooms chat, their voices low,
Plotting pranks in a secret show.
'Who can dress as a gnome the best?'
While snails judge, in striped vests.

In the busyness of life below,
A party forms for all to know.
With twirling spores and glittering lights,
They jam the night with happy sights.

As fungi laugh and they unite,
In merry jest, they greet the night.
The city blooms with tales so bright,
In every laugh, a spore takes flight.

The Unseen Hums of the Ecosystem

Whispers float through leafy greens,
A buzzing leaf tells quirky scenes.
'Hey, who stole my sunshine snack?'
A wise old tree, 'It's time to track!'

Underfoot, the ground's alive,
Where ants convene and gossip thrive.
A cricket strums a tune so fine,
While beetles boast of epic climbs.

The wind, it tickles blades with glee,
As bees debate, 'Is this the key?'
Mice tell tales of moonlit feats,
While spiders weave their clever beats.

In this realm, the characters play,
Sing songs of life, both night and day.
With every hum, a joke unwinds,
In unseen realms, the fun it finds.

Echoes in the Green Abyss

In a patch of moss, so cozy and bright,
A squirrel plays chess with a soft pillow fight.
Mushrooms are judges, with fungi as cheers,
While snails in their shells offer terrible jeers.

Beneath leafy hats, there's laughter and glee,
A rabbit in glasses is reading a tree.
The ants form a line for the dance of the year,
With beetles performing, they all sip on beer.

Frogs croak a tune that would shatter the night,
But toads on a pogo stick win every fight.
With dragonflies buzzing, the scene is absurd,
As a worm sings a ballad, completely unheard.

The shadows all giggle, enchanting the scene,
Dancing with shadows, a sight to be seen.
So join in the fun, let your worries all fade,
In this nutty domain where the critters have played.

Nightfall's Embrace in the Thicket

Under the stars, where the shadows convene,
A raccoon in a tuxedo presents quite the scene.
The owls all are judges, with wise, widening eyes,
As the fireflies drum in a shimmering rise.

Hedgehogs in top hats glide past with a spin,
While moles do the twist, saying, 'Let's begin!'
A hedgehog named Harold calls out for a snack,
Creating a banquet of crumbs from his pack.

The whispers of leaves are the music tonight,
As dancing chipmunks twist in pure delight.
The moon chuckles softly, illuminating fun,
As crickets play violin for everyone.

So, twirl with the owls and waltz with the moss,
For in this dark thicket, there's never a loss.
Laughter and joy float on cool evening air,
In a world where the night wears a jubilant flair.

Life Between the Nebulous Shadows

In the gaps of the leaves, where the shadows convene,
A platypus juggles and plays on a screen.
The twinkling lights flutter, like stars on a spree,
As chipmunks do flips, all the critters agree.

A turtle in flip-flops talks fashion and style,
While bugs on the sidelines all giggle awhile.
A squirrel with a beard spins tales of delight,
As the mice start a chorus, 'The worm cannot write!'

Beneath tangled vines, there's a party of sorts,
With raccoons in capes and a dance of retorts.
The shadows make faces, while mushrooms can't hide,
In this playful realm where the oddballs collide.

So join with the laughter, lose track of the time,
In the whimsical dance, let your spirit unwind.
Within nebulous shadows, pure joy will unbind,
As the humor of nature leaves all woes behind.

Stories from the Ground's Embrace

Gather 'round for stories from dirt and from dread,
Where even the dirtworms can argue in bed.
A grasshopper named Joe takes the mic as he sings,
While ants provide backup, with their wiggly flings.

The rocks start to chuckle, with tales of their past,
Of thunderous storms and how long they can last.
A lizard in glasses recites funny quotes,
As rabbits in bowties bring up ancient notes.

Down by the roots where the whispers take form,
A turtle spins yarns, with an unyielding charm.
The creatures all gather 'round laughter and cheer,
For in tales from the ground, there's nothing to fear.

So come share your tales, let your laughter ignite,
In the world of the wild, it's a whimsical night.
From dirt to the trees, let your spirit be free,
In these stories of joy, there's always more tea!

Whispers Beneath the Canopy

Tiny critters hold a meeting,
With acorns stacked, there's no competing.
Squirrels play poker with old tree bark,
While mushrooms gossip till it gets dark.

Frogs prank the birds with silly songs,
And raccoons' dance parties last too long.
A worm dressed as a dapper gent,
Sways to tunes the beetles invent.

Ladybugs jam with spiders' webs,
Throwing wild parties with their celeb pebs.
Grasshoppers join with a skyline groove,
Making sure that the leaves all move.

Ants in tuxedos lead the parade,
While butterflies flutter, unafraid.
Every critter winks with delight,
In this fun world, everything's light!

Secrets of the Leafy Underworld

Underneath leaves, a secret's known,
Where gnomes sip tea on a toadstool throne.
With their tiny hats and jovial laughs,
Crafting plans no one else can grasp.

A hedgehog's story makes all hearts soar,
About a snail who wanted to explore.
He rode on a leaf with flair and speed,
While critters cheered, "That's the life indeed!"

Mice build a castle from twigs and fluff,
Claiming their realm, they've got the right stuff.
Squeaky guards shout, "All hail the queen!"
As the world marvels at their grand scene.

Fireflies glow for the evening show,
As the moon grins down, with a soft glow.
They twirl and swirl in the soft night air,
While the trees chuckle, unaware of the flair.

Tales from the Woodland Bed

In the thicket, beds of moss and fluff,
Critters snuggle tight, but it's never enough.
Bunnies snore loudly, while hedgehogs sigh,
Dreaming of pizza that floats in the sky.

When twilight fades into deep night shades,
Chipmunks host parties that rival parades.
Raccoons juggle under the soft moonlight,
While snails do the limbo—what a funny sight!

Tales of the wily fox on the run,
With a hat made from leaves just to have fun.
He slipped on a branch and fell with a thud,
And laughed as he landed right into a mud.

A turtle who sings through the night, oh dear,
Croaking out ballads that all want to hear.
With each fancy note, the world starts to sway,
Creating sweet dreams till the break of day.

Shadows of the Earthbound Realm

In shadows where the wild things play,
A dance-off springs up at the end of the day.
With ants in sneakers doing the twist,
As a deer presides, you can't let them miss.

Beetles breakdance on pebbles so round,
While a shy owl hoots a delightful sound.
Every trunk's a stage, every leaf a fan,
As the hedgehogs cheer for their best plan.

Twinkling lights guide through the leafy maze,
With fireflies winking in the moon's soft glaze.
Mice form a band with sticks and stones,
Making melodies from old, forgotten tones.

The shadows giggle, they can't keep still,
As laughter and music bring life to the hill.
Each creature adds magic to the fun tale,
In this mischievous world where friendship prevails.

The Symphony of Silent Sprouts

Tiny greens dance and sway,
Wearing hats of dew all day.
Whispers tickle, roots have fun,
Playing hide and seek—who's won?

Ants march in a grand parade,
Chasing crumbs they've deftly made.
The mushrooms giggle, prance around,
A secret world beneath the ground.

Ladybugs join in the jest,
Wearing spots, they think they're best.
Frogs in chorus croak with glee,
Singing tunes of jubilee.

As the sun begins to fade,
Worms compose their own charade.
With a wink and playful nod,
Life grows wild—oh, how they prod!

Moonlit Paths of the Underbrush

Underneath the glowing sky,
Hedgehogs giggle as they try.
Rabbits leap with carefree bliss,
In shadows cast, they chase and kiss.

Owls bring jokes from tree to tree,
Hooting laughter, can't you see?
A squirrel swirls in twirls so neat,
Circuiting a mossy seat.

The fireflies spark a disco light,
Dancing wildly through the night.
Beneath the cloak of silvery beams,
They twirl in nature's fanciful dreams.

As night drapes over every nook,
Raccoons gather 'round the cook.
They feast on snacks—oh, the delight,
In the moonlit paths, all feels right!

The Lullaby of Hidden Hollows

In the nooks where shadows dwell,
Whispering willows weave a spell.
Crickets chirp their sleepy tune,
While toads croak beneath the moon.

Bunnies stretch with dreamy sighs,
Cuddled close beneath the skies.
Hedgehogs snore with tiny snores,
Nestled deep in earthy floors.

Squirrels yawn and softly sway,
Bedtime stories on display.
The branches sway with sweet embrace,
As dreams repair this cozy space.

As slumber falls, the hush persists,
With giggles faint among the mist.
Nature hums her gentle lore,
In hidden hollows, fun galore!

Mycelium Serenades

In the damp and leafy gloom,
Fungi flourish, learn to bloom.
The mycelium sings with flair,
Tickles roots and fills the air.

Ticklish toes of little sprites,
Bouncing under mushroom lights.
Wiggly worms join the show,
Underneath, they put on a glow.

Wanderlust in every spore,
They've got fun planned—always more!
The laughter echoes, whispers spread,
Dancing dreams where none have tread.

With a twirl and jumpy cheer,
Nature jests, we laugh and sneer.
In this world of jokes and plays,
The mycelium serenades!

Shades of Dreams Among the Roots

Beneath the leaves, where shadows play,
A squirrel dances, all in dismay.
He thinks he's stealthy, then trips on a twig,
And lands in a puddle like a big, floppy pig.

A bug in a suit gives a speech to the flies,
While flowers nod gently, rolling their eyes.
The acorns giggle, tucked safe in their shells,
As mushrooms share secrets that no one else tells.

A snail with a cape claims to glide through the air,
But inch by inch, it takes ages, I swear.
A tiny parade of ants marches by,
Waving their antennae, oh me, oh my!

So linger a bit where the wild things jest,
Amidst these delights, nature's comical fest.
Each step that you take pulls laughter from roots,
In this whimsical realm where goofiness shoots.

The Lush Tapestry of Life Below

In the damp and dark, where giggles abound,
A raccoon plays poker with chips from the ground.
He raises his paw while the shadows all laugh,
Claiming his winnings — a really big half!

A hedgehog in shades is the coolest of cats,
Strumming a ukelele, with some witty quats.
The daisies all sway, tapping toes in delight,
As crickets compose tunes that last through the night.

The earthworms are counting their twisty old hats,
While beetles debate the best way to strut.
They prance in a line, oh the joy of it all,
As butterflies chuckle, "Look at them crawl!"

This lively underworld, tucked cozy and neat,
Is a carnival realm where funny things meet.
And if you get lost in this quirky ballet,
Just follow the laughter, it's sure to lead the way!

Whimsies in the Understory

In bustling lanes where the ferns hang low,
A beetle recites poetry, putting on a show.
With each little verse, the mushrooms all cheer,
As fireflies twinkle, "Best poem of the year!"

A jolly old toad croaks a popular tune,
While turtles join in, shifting under the moon.
They've got a dance step that's truly unique,
You'd laugh till you cry, oh, the rhythm they seek!

Elves with wild hair gather acorns for fun,
They juggle them high, a delightful run.
But just look out, for a cheeky big fox,
Who'll swipe all their treats, yelling, "I love these blocks!"

With giggles abounding and joy in the cracks,
Adventures pop up like whimsical snacks.
So come take a peek in this playful embrace,
Where mishaps are treasures, and mishaps a race!

Whirls of Fern and Feather

Down where the sunlight peeks shyly through,
An owl's on a skateboard, how about you?
He tries to look cool, but then takes a spill,
And flaps off in style, with a feathered thrill!

A party of frogs plays hopscotch by streams,
Each jump turns to laughter, or so it seems.
One slips on a lily, and it causes a splash,
They giggle and croak, it's a belly-flop bash!

The snail with a beret and tiny round shades,
Wanders with flair in the soft, leafy glades.
"Today's a good day to show off my style,"
Said the sloth, who contemplated it for a while.

In this bustling world where the silly come forth,
Nature's own cartoon, bursting with mirth.
So tiptoe through whispers of laughter and cheer,
And toast to the wonders that flourish down here!

The Alchemy of Mushrooms and Moonlight

In shadows where the toadstools shine,
A party starts with herbs and wine.
The fairies dance with glee in sight,
They twirl around in silver light.

A gnome forgot his hat one day,
Now squirrels wear it, what a play!
He grumbles loud, but can't complain,
At least his head's not wet with rain.

The nightingale sings songs of cheer,
While hedgehogs sip their froggy beer.
With mushrooms stacked in funny shapes,
The laughter echoes, joy escapes.

Beware the mushrooms with a grin,
They might just pull you in and spin!
In moonlight's glow, we lose our cares,
As stepping stones become the stairs.

Sylvan Whispers of the Forgotten

Old roots weave tales from long ago,
Where acorns trade in secrets low.
The owls connive with peppered winks,
Sharing laughs over squirrel drinks.

A lost shoe hangs on a crooked branch,
A sign of a dance or a wild ranch.
While rabbits giggle in the night,
A snail breaks out a disco light.

The breeze carries tales, quirks abound,
As fireflies throw a silent sound.
"Who dropped the acorns?" whispers grow,
"Who needs them all? It's just for show!"

Yet nature's laughter fills the air,
With every rustle, life's a fair.
Forgotten songs in shadows creep,
As woodland secrets love to leap.

Tales from the Underbrush

Beneath the leaves, the critters plot,
A masquerade of scurries and thought.
The ants bring pizza, the rabbits snack,
While moles share stories from the track.

A turtle joins, a hat askew,
"I'm late!" he says, "What's wrong with you?"
The laughter peals like bells at play,
As everyone joins the milking bay.

The friendships bloom in tangled knots,
Amidst the jumbled gears and lots.
They tell of giants lurking near,
Yet offer pie as streams draw near.

In underbrush, the mischief brews,
With every rustle, secret clues.
This merry band of worms and bees,
Dances beneath the swaying trees.

The Art of Camouflage in Green

A chameleon on an emerald throne,
Reads leafy books on his own.
"Blend in, they say," he often scoffs,
"What's wrong with bright? Let's shake it off!"

While frogs in T-shirts spill some paint,
On crickets who just love to faint.
"Your speckles clash!" the toad complains,
As all of nature laughs and reigns.

The hedgehogs wear their spiky suits,
While butterflies refuse their boots.
"Fashion's fierce!" a deer proclaims,
As shadows dance to festive games.

So here we laugh in leafy hues,
While all the critters take their views.
In concerts held beneath the leaves,
Nature's style, oh how it weaves!

Buds of Mystery and Wonder

In the thicket, secrets weave,
Tiny critters, tricks up their sleeve.
Mushrooms giggle, ants dance a jig,
Who knew the wild could be so big?

Squirrels plotting in the low branches,
Inventing games with funny glances.
The flowers gossip, oh what a sight,
Tales of bees and their airborne flight.

A leaf drops down, oh what a quirk,
It lands on a snail, who quivers with work.
Down below, the shadows play,
Jokes of nature brighten the day.

Rustling Through the Wild Undergrowth

Beneath the fronds, a party stirs,
A hedgehog smiles, causing a blur.
Frogs croak tales of daring feats,
While rabbits hop on their tiny beats.

A raccoon juggles acorns with flair,
While owls chuckle from high up there.
The grasshoppers leap in lively rows,
Every jump a chance to pose.

Crickets chirp with a rhythmic beat,
As they tap dance on tiny feet.
Surprises hide in every nook,
Get ready for the wildest book.

Veils of Fog over Life's Thickets

In the mist, the world looks sly,
Where shadows giggle and twirl up high.
A fox in glasses reads the news,
His jests in riddles, playful clues.

Fogs swim like blankets, soft and gray,
Hiding antics that might betray.
An owl winks with a wise old grin,
"Join the fun; it's where we begin!"

Each tree a trickster, roots stretch and curl,
A world of mischief begins to swirl.
Leaves whisper secrets behind their backs,
Laughter floats through the leafy cracks.

Murmurs of the Wooded Realm

Among the trees, a chorus hums,
Voices of nature—droning drums.
Bears brew tea with honey bees,
While woodpeckers play the harmonies.

Mice tell tales of grand escapades,
Chasing shadows in leafy glades.
Underfoot, a sprightly deer,
Cracks a joke and disappears.

The winds carry giggles, crisp and sweet,
As flowers swap shoes on tiny feet.
Every rustle is a laugh shared,
In this realm, no heart feels scared.

Secret Lives of the Undergrowth

Beneath the leaves, what do we find?
Squirrels juggling acorns, oh so blind.
Worms in top hats, strutting with flair,
Toadstools gossiping about the air.

Ants hosting parties, dancing in lines,
Beetles debating the best punchlines.
A raccoon's orchestra, quite the show,
While foxes bet on who'll steal the dough.

Under thickets, secrets abound,
With laughter echoed, a merry sound.
A tiny snail plays music so sweet,
As rabbits plan the next grand feast.

In this wild chaos, who keeps score?
The mushrooms chuckle, "We want more!"
With every creature, a jest or two,
In this hidden world, laughter rings true.

The Lost Chronicles of Woodland Shadows

In the twilight, shadows dance wide,
A hedgehog spins tales with great pride.
While owls perch high, they hoot in glee,
"Guess who tripped over that old tree?"

Mice in cloaks with secrets to share,
Adventures whispered on cool night air.
Squirrels plotting the next big heist,
"Who stole my snack? It's not very nice!"

Beneath the moon, a contest unfolds,
Who can do tricks? The tale is retold.
With fireflies bringing the disco lights,
Crickets providing those funky bites.

The chatter rises, the night wears on,
With a final giggle, the dawn is drawn.
And as the sun smiles from above,
The woodland chuckles, a world to love.

Layers of Life Beneath the Bark

Peeking under the bark, what delight,
A ticklish tick grows a spider's bite.
Ants in a line, a parade so grand,
While beetles play chess on the leaf-clad land.

Mushrooms with hats from a party last week,
With whispers of gossip, they all squeak.
Snails in a hurry, "I'm late!" they declare,
While worms throw confetti in earthy air.

Twirling in dance, the roots can't resist,
"Join the fun, it's something you've missed!"
With a nutty acorn, they all strike a pose,
Creating a scene where the laughter just flows.

So next time you tread, take a peek and see,
The giggles and grins in this jolly spree.
For life beneath bark is wild and bright,
With joyful creatures bringing pure delight.

Enigma of the Ground's Embrace

In the embrace of earth, a puzzling sight,
A mole that moonwalks under the night.
The crickets tell tales with a comedic flair,
While rabbits are caught in a game of hair.

Under twigs, secrets hidden away,
They plot future pranks for the break of day.
With whispers and giggles, the shadows all meet,
To share in the laughter of life at their feet.

A picnic of ants with crumbs they carry,
While ladybugs fret, "Who lost the cherry?"
Bees buzz in rhythm, their jokes take flight,
Creating confusion in morning light.

So wander the path where the wild things roam,
And join in the fun of their leafy home.
For in every crevice and crack you adore,
Lies a world full of laughter, forevermore.

Mossy Dreams and Hidden Streams

Mice in tiny hats roam free,
Chasing cheese with glee,
Frogs with banjos strum away,
Dancing by the creek, hooray!

Mossy beds, a cushy sight,
Squirrels giggle through the night,
Raccoons play hide and seek,
In a game, so unique!

A frog hops up, says hello,
Offers snacks, a fun show,
Butterflies break out in song,
Join the fun, come along!

Stars above, they twinkle bright,
Creatures gather, pure delight,
In this land, where laughers gleam,
Whimsical is the dream!

The Lullaby of Fallen Leaves

Leaves tumble down, a giggling crew,
Whispering secrets, just for you,
Caterpillars on parade,
Wearing hats that seem handmade!

Chirping crickets keep the beat,
While ants tap dance on tiny feet,
A ladybug leads a conga line,
In this world, everything's fine!

A hiccup from the trees so tall,
As acorns bounce and squirrels fall,
Mushrooms caper, slightly spry,
As slapstick fungi fly by!

In this rustling, cozy place,
Laughter gathers, fills the space,
As moonlight sprinkles in between,
The quirkiest scene you've seen!

Enchanted Echoes of Twilight

Bats wear capes, the night is young,
Cheesy jokes on tongues are sung,
In the shadows, giggles creep,
Mice are plotting as they sweep!

Fireflies blink in silly patterns,
While tadpoles make the best of hatters,
A raccoon tries to juggle leaves,
Dropping them—oh, how he grieves!

Whispers drift on twilight air,
As owls play poker without care,
Frogs read fortunes in the mud,
Predicting fun in every thud!

Stars burst forth in joyful cheers,
As laughter flows from tiny peers,
In this twilight, joy will soar,
Echoes dance—who could ask for more?

Beneath the Bark, Tales Untold

Beneath the bark, a party brews,
Worms share tales of late-night snooze,
Beetles clink their tiny cups,
While gophers tell of daring jumps!

A wise old owl stirs up the fun,
Sharing jokes till day is done,
Fungi giggle, what a sight,
Spinning tales under the moonlight!

In the hollow, acorns play games,
Each one whispered some crazy names,
A bashful toad sums it all,
Saying, "Join us, come, don't stall!"

With every chuckle, secrets grow,
As adventures weave and flow,
In this world beneath the bark,
Magic dances, bright and stark!

Tales Untold

Squirrels gather with popcorn, bright,
Telling tales of their wild flight,
Chasing tails in circles wide,
While a hedgehog can't help but glide!

A chipmunk's quirks are the best,
His riddle's jest beats all the rest,
As bugs applaud with tiny hands,
In this realm of silly plans!

Under mushrooms soft and round,
Giggles bounce from ground to ground,
Elves with sparkling shoes pirouette,
Creating chaos—no regret!

When twilight fades, the moon will cheer,
For brighter tales draw ever near,
In this lively, wacky sphere,
Fun and laughter, come, don't fear!

Fables from the Verdant Veil

A squirrel wore a hat of fluff,
He danced about, a little gruff.
The mushrooms giggled, hid their glee,
And said, "He's not as smart as he seems to be!"

A rabbit joined the jig with flair,
His ears flopped wildly in the air.
The hedgehogs rolled, they laughed so bold,
"The dance-off's won, or so we're told!"

A wise old owl asked with a hoot,
"Who turned the dirt into a suit?"
The crickets chirped a silly tune,
While waltzing 'neath a silver moon.

So gather 'round, join in the jest,
In nature's ring, we all feel blessed.
With each laugh shared, and antics grand,
Life's just a game in this green land!

The Stolen Breath of the Natural World

A cheeky breeze blew through the trees,
It whispered secrets, made us freeze.
The flowers shrugged, "What's with the chill?"
"Was it the deer, or was it Will?"

The frogs complained, "It's not our fault,
That butterfly stole our cozy vault!"
With fluttering wings, it flew away,
Leaving the pond in disarray.

A raccoon grinned, "Let's turn this round,
I've got a plan that will astound!
We'll draw the breath back in a scoop,
And host a party with the whole troop!"

So laughter rang through air and leaf,
As chaos turned to comic relief.
In nature's realm so wildly spun,
The stolen breath, now shared for fun!

Beneath the Canopy: A Hidden Realm

Beneath the leafy hats so wide,
Lies a very loopy side.
The ants parade, all in a row,
"Oh, look! We found a treasure, don't you know?"

A snail stood up and struck a pose,
"Check out my shell, it's quite the rose!"
The beetles chuckled, rolled on ground,
"And here we thought, you'd lost, not found!"

A dance began with wiggles tight,
As goofy creatures twirled in spite.
The moss then hummed a quirky beat,
While everyone tapped their silly feet.

So wander deep where laughter glows,
In giddy realms where nature flows.
Amid the fun and joyous spree,
You'll find the heart of jubilee!

Dreams Entwined with Twigs and Moss

A tiny mouse with dreams so big,
Wore a crown made of a twig.
She whispered softly, "Watch me soar,
In dreams I'm more than just a chore!"

The snails conspired, "Let's build a tower,
With bits of grass and a sprinkle of flower!"
But just as they took the first step,
A squirrel giggled, "No strength, just pep!"

With moonlight's glow and dreams in sight,
They crafted a fort that felt just right.
A party formed of twigs and laughs,
In the sunset's glow, they danced like chaffs.

So gather all, let joy entwine,
In quirky sets where spirits shine.
With twigs and moss, and laughter rife,
In this dreamland, we embrace life!

www.ingramcontent.com/pod-product-compliance
Lightning Source LLC
Chambersburg PA
CBHW071840160426
43209CB00003B/368